Love and Destiny

Anthony T. Padovano

Love and Destiny

PAULIST PRESS
New York/Mahwah

Library of Congress Cataloging-in-Publication Data.

Padovano, Anthony T.
   Love and destiny.

   1. Marriage—Religious aspects—Catholic Church.
2. Catholic Church—Doctrines.   I.   Title.
BX2250.P32   1987   248.8′4   87-8862
ISBN 0-8091-2895-0 (pbk.)

Published by Paulist Press
997 Macarthur Boulevard
Mahwah, New Jersey 07430

Printed and bound in the
United States of America

Contents

Preface 1

1/ Intimacy and Fidelity 3

2/ Sexual Love and Sacramental Life.............. 12

3/ Children and Hope for the World.............. 21

4/ The God of Leisure, The Christ of Laughter... 30

5/ Rituals and Memories 39

6/ Careers and Money, Commitments and
   Frugality 49

7/ Failure and Forgiveness 59

8/ All That Is Freely Given Is Never Lost 68

9/ We Shall Meet Again 78

FOR THERESA
WHO HAS MADE HER WORLD A SACRAMENT
SO THAT ALL WHO ENTER IT RECEIVE GRACE

Preface

In many ways, it is the ultimate mystery, the culminating grace. The human family may differ on all other issues but on this it reaches an impressive consensus, that marriage is the most important thing we do. We are born from marriages, we give almost all our adult years to them, we hope to end life with our families near us.

The greatest and most demanding of all human accomplishments may be a good marriage. Nothing else brings more joy to human life or causes more pain when it falters.

The Bible begins its story with an account of creation. When human life is brought into existence, it is considered the finest work of God. The first gift God provides for the human family is not religion or guidelines, liturgy or ethics. It is marriage.

On every side, we are reminded that we have been made for marriage. Social structures and psychological needs, anatomy and chemistry, language and law are shaped by the priority of marriage. Nothing human beings do is more charged with meaning than marriage. Religion exists only because marriage precedes it. The future is assured not by massive sacred and secular institutions but because people want to belong to human families and struggle to make the planet a fit place for them.

When we are tempted to despair, we need only attend a wedding or a birth, we need only observe a family's rituals of survival and affection, we need only reflect on how much people do to make their relationships succeed, and we begin to hope again.

People will never stop loving or creating life. They will be generous often with those bound to them by commitments and by flesh and blood. There is no justification for despair.

Hope is not an abstraction. It is as concrete as marriage, as permanent as family ties, as joyful as love, as near as an embrace, as personal as pain, as exuberant as freedom.

A book on marriage is not a book about a subject of no interest to us. In marriage, our humanity is at stake. When marriage is neglected, society is irreversibly wounded and the Church is fundamentally weakened. Marriage is the primary sacrament of relationship and love. All other sacraments emerge from it.

A book on marriage is a book about the values people sacrifice the most for and cherish ardently. Marriage is a commitment to life as far as it goes and for as long as it endures.

Chapter One

Intimacy and Fidelity

Without intimacy, there is no fidelity.

Intimacy occurs when we perceive trust and become vulnerable before it. It is an intuition or feeling. It is a revelation of the self to another.

Fidelity is the capacity to assume responsibility for someone whose intimacy we have received. It preserves the trust which has occurred between two people.

Fidelity occurs between two people, not between a person and an institution.

We are not expected to be faithful to marriage as an institution but, rather, to the wife or husband who has become vulnerable to us.

Institutions do not become vulnerable or intimate with their members. We cannot, strictly speaking, become faithful to them. Institutions seek consistency and conformity; people exchange intimacy and fidelity.

There are a number of factors which make intimacy difficult for people.

3

Fear

The most important of these may be fear of ourselves.

It is not an easy thing to be a human being. It is
even more frightening to become a particular person,
different from all others. The stranger we most fear in
life is ourselves. The most formidable of all persons to
accept is ourselves.

In years of counseling people, I have been aston-
ished at how low an opinion people generally have
about themselves.

Nothing deteriorates a marriage more relentlessly
and thoroughly than the conviction that we are of no
worth. It seems crucial, therefore, to deal with this issue before we discuss any other.

Why is self-acceptance so arduous?

Responsibility

Life is not only a gift but a demand, not only a
grace but a responsibility. On some levels of awareness, we realize that life is more than we can handle,
that the height and depth, the variety and diversity of
life are simply overwhelming. It is remarkable that we
do as well as we do.

Every day of our lives we are given light and
nourishment, air and water, friends and memories,
love and flowers, stars and darkness, greetings and
embraces, sleep and dreams. The list can, of course,
be extended indefinitely.

We become indifferent to much of this but cumulatively we realize that we do not deserve, that we have not earned, that we are not worthy of all that we experience.

When we encounter the love which leads us to marriage we sense this unworthiness most keenly. But it has been there all along. When people are generous with us, our immediate response is bewilderment: "Why would you do this for me? Who am I?"

Conversely, we feel we deserve the reverses and failures, the afflictions and punishments of life. We object in public to the fact that this should not have happened to us but, in private, we convince ourselves that the retribution was long overdue. We search our lives for the sins which called disaster down upon us. And we usually find them.

In spiritual fatigue and physical exhaustion, we begin to believe we are of no account, that we were always nobody. We reduce ourselves to anonymity.

When divorce terminates a marriage, people seek a place to hide, not only because the pain hurts so much but because, in shame, they blame themselves, excessively, repeatedly. We are ready to believe the worst of ourselves.

Gift

It is difficult to live with the idea that life is given to us freely and abundantly; our society insists, instead, on merit, earning one's way, self-reliance.

The truth of the matter is that everything in life which holds it together and allows it to continue is given. One does not earn a friend or a child, a parent or a future, humor or companionship, grace and God. They are simply given.

Indeed, we do not even fully earn that which seems most of all the result of our efforts, namely, money and material possessions. Other people work harder for less; others work less for more. There seems to be a random character to the way life functions. Some are born blind and some die poor; some inherit intelligence and some receive wealth; some are male and some are female.

Our society believes that life is a process of earning our way but, in our hearts, we know it is not.

Society can make us feel guilty when we are disadvantaged, even though the disadvantages are arbitrary. Poverty is a relative term and blindness afflicts us all; intelligence is often measured by marketability and credentials rather than by native endowment; cultures are enriched in more ways than their gross national product indicates; gender gives and withholds opportunities which have nothing to do with personal worth.

An adequate response to all of this is acceptance of the conditions which surround our life without always assuming responsibility for them. Many things are simply as they are and there is no changing them.

Jesus told us that our anxiety and fretting would not add an inch to our height.

Creative Acceptance

Some of life is initiative and effort but most of it is creative acceptance. Even our marriages are less our

6

doing than we think. Some people work hard at marriages that fail; others work little at marriages that succeed. There may be an element of luck or good fortune, randomness, if you will, in marriage that is easily overlooked. All the planning and energy we are capable of cannot assure a marriage. This does not mean that preparation and sacrifice are not necessary or that they do not limit the risk. But there are no guarantees. And so, marriage is acceptance to a considerable degree. We have no right to claim full credit for marriages that are happy nor to blame ourselves totally for marriages that bring misery. Self-righteousness, on the one hand, and self-punishment, on the other, are not justified.

Creative acceptance means that we learn to love those things about us we cannot change since they are part and parcel of who we are. A liability in one area of our life helps develop an asset in another. A weakness in one person attracts the strength of another person to us. The person who loves us and wishes to marry us would not be with us unless all the circumstances, even those we most regretted, had made us the person we are.

Who is to say what the best circumstances for life's development are? We once thought education and affluence, culture and religion, health and intelligence, beauty and youth would assure happiness and worth. Evil, like a weed, however, takes root in the most unlikely places.

The American novelist, Henry James, tells us in *Portrait of a Lady* about a young woman who had all the advantages. Although she embodied the American dream, she did not find contentment or love. Her marriage was a source of misery. Human beings are not so mechanical or predictable that one can guarantee success with pre-arranged supposedly ideal circumstances.

Ideals

The truth of the matter is that there are no ideal circumstances. There are only concrete experiences. Jesus had trouble with those of his contemporaries who thought they had it all. He brought grace instead to those who had nothing and who became grateful for anything.

Intimacy is nurtured in a grateful heart, one which rejoices in the goodness of life and believes there is a purpose in the pain. Gratitude is the sign that one is not threatened by one's own vulnerability. Gratitude means that one is able to receive a gift without demanding that one be worthy first and without feeling that one is totally undeserving.

Intimacy is our capacity to listen to the life story of another, to hear it without judgment, to receive it without measuring it against a more ideal life. Intimacy allows me to tell my own story to someone I know will not violate it, to someone who will not force me to make a fiction of my life, to someone who will keep sacred the memory and the meaning of my identity.

There is a dark, destructive side to each of us. This too needs naming and telling. The secret sins, the buried regrets, the painful shame are part of the story.

It may well be that there is no one person who will be able to absorb the entire story. There are those who are receptive to some truths but are not ready for others.

It is also ill-advised to become intimate with everyone. Intimacy entails responsibility; we cannot make everyone responsible for all that is vulnerable and sacred in us.

If no one may be able to absorb all our story, if everyone ought not be made to hear it, there are always those few who know as much about us as we are able to communicate. A good marriage requires total intimacy or as close to that as we can come.

If we preserve others from all that is ignoble in us, we deny the other the opportunity to care for us and to become more deeply one with us. The strength of the marital bond depends upon how effectively we allow ourselves to become weak before the other.

Perfectionism

The greatest enemy of intimacy is the demon of perfectionism. If we believe that we can be lovable only when we are perfect, if we suppose we can only love someone who is already perfect, then the marriage we enter is doomed from the start, destined for divorce or stagnation.

Every flaw in one's marital partner is already present in the other to some degree. No one of us has mastered any one value perfectly. It may be that infidelity takes one form in one partner and a different form in the other. The tensions that can arise in a marriage over money and control, sex and children, relatives and careers are not present totally in one spouse as a problem and entirely absent from the other. Every flaw in the other is a reflection of the same flaw in us at a different stage of development. When we receive and forgive the other, we accept and forgive ourselves.

Intimacy is a great adventure, a deeply satisfying human experience, a liberating and joyous discovery. Nothing we do is more rewarding than our relationship with people to whom we are bonded, with whom we are intimate, for whom we are ready to sacrifice everything, in whom the meaning of our life has been entrusted.

Fidelity

Intimacy is the key to fidelity. Before people can become faithful to us, they must know the person to whom their faithfulness is given. When we accept the other on intimate terms, we agree to be responsible for that person. This responsibility is not a substitute for the autonomous life of the other but a willingness on our part to be faithful to the sacred dimensions of another life entrusted to our keeping.

Fidelity in marriage endures as long as intimacy is maintained. This fidelity, therefore, is not the work of one person but the achievement of the couple.

Each needs to be courageous with intimacy and trusting with vulnerability. In this scheme of things, infidelity to the other becomes infidelity with one's own self. If we are not trustworthy with the self-donation of the other, a donation we encouraged by receiving intimacy, then we are unreliable with our own life. Even if the marriage terminates in divorce, elements of trust and faithfulness must be maintained. If there is a violation in these areas, the unfaithful spouse is also damaged.

And so intimacy and fidelity are different steps in the same dance. It is a dance in which giving and receiving, intimacy and fidelity create the music of love, the harmony of a shared life, the melody of marriage.

It is a remarkable experience to encounter oneself in the other and to discover that one is no longer a stranger to one's own self.

Such a dance is a cosmic dance, even a divine dance. For it is God who gave us to ourselves and made love in the world so that we would not be alone. It is God who was intimate with us when we were frightened and faithful to us when fidelity to ourselves was more than we could handle.

It is God who forgave us when we were lost beyond repair. It is God who listened to the story and heard our heart from the time we were in our mother's womb until death seemed to silence the story and our heart forever. It is God who has been faithful to the integrity and texture of our life narrative. God preserved us from arrogance in our goodness and despair in our darkness.

It is God we meet in each other when we love.

Fidelity keeps faith with ourselves and with the other, with human and divine intimacy, with all that is holy in life and sacred in each one of us.

Chapter Two

Sexual Love and Sacramental Life

It begins with touching. Life occurs because we touch each other.

When we no longer touch, life withers. Love is unsatisfied with distance.

Intimacy reaches its total expression when a communion of hearts becomes a bonding of bodies. At this point, fidelity passes over from being trustworthy with the vulnerability of another to becoming a united life with the other. The life that occurs in this touching is not only the life conceived from sexual love but the life of the couple sealed in sexual union. The two lovers are coupled for life, not only in the sense that they intend the union to last but also because the union is on the side of life. It endures and it gives life.

The moment of conception is the result of sexual love and the first moment in the sexual life of the child. No other single genetic factor influences our future more than the gender we become.

The touching which set the conception in motion leads to further touching in fertilization as the elements of life fuse. This fusion is a symbol of the sexual union of the couple and it brings life to another person.

The touching of sexual intercourse is complemented by the touching of implantation, adhering, clinging to the body of the mother. The new child cannot see or hear, taste or smell. It touches and this touching assures its life.

Touching gives us an intense experience of presence and it provides us with a future. It is the one sense we do not lose during life. Sight and sound, smell and taste may wither but touch is with us from the first moment to the final hour.

It is possible to live a full life without the other senses. But when our capacity to perceive touch is gone, we are beyond human reach and near death itself.

Touch gives life and takes it away. Contact with a lethal substance frequently brings death; the other senses can perceive a deadly substance with immunity. Touching something dangerous, however, is often more than life can handle. It is as though reality enters us through touch more immediately than by any other sense. We become what we touch. If there is death, so to speak, in the things we handle, death seizes us.

Life not only originates in touching but develops as touching heals us and renews us. Holding hands and embracing, kissing and caressing bring love more directly to us than any other sense. The sight and sound of those we love are thrilling but they prompt us to stretch out our arms to touch them. It is then that the meeting is complete.

It is tragic when two lovers behold each other at a distance, capable of seeing and hearing but prevented from touching.

The texture of love and the shape of life are perceived in touching. When a friendship or a marriage ends, the death of that experience is described in terms associated with touching. The couple is "separated"; the lovers are "torn" from each other; death "takes us away."

The Body

It is useful, therefore, to reflect on the meaning of the body. The body is the root or radical, the first and last sacrament. A sacrament is a physical reality which brings us into a relationship with the deeper dimensions of life, eventually with God.

These thoughts require explanation. Let us begin by observing that the human body is a sacred experience. It is holy in its every fiber.

Few people know this better than parents. The body of a baby is an object of indescribable awe. Most people have their most intense religious experience, their most convincing assurance of God in holding their new-born children.

Lovers know this also. The nearness of the lover is a source of endless joy. Lovers know that the touching of hands and the embrace of affection are gifts that cannot be exhausted. We need nothing more to put us in touch with God than the touch of those we love.

The body is the basis for all we know and value in the sacramental life.

Genesis and Gender

When God made the world, men and women were fashioned as images of their Creator. This truth is expressed at the beginning of the Bible in unforgettable language.

This likeness to God is rooted in our bodies and in our genders. It is true, of course, that reason and imagination, freedom and love have no physical shape. They are "spiritual" realities. And they are also convincing signs of our similarity to God.

But scripture does not speak of these in the creation story. It describes the whole person, especially the body and gender, as the handiwork of God. God creates them "male and female" and gives them to each other as a sexual experience. Somewhere in the majesty of our bodies and in the mystery of our sexual identities, God dwells.

In the second chapter of Genesis, God is graphically involved with the physical making of human life. The first man is molded from dust and clay. Even the more "spiritual" action of breathing into the first man intends the animation of a body.

We are not suggesting that human life images God only in the body. We are affirming, however, that it is inadequate to believe we are like God only in our "spiritual" functioning.

The physical emphasis is intensified as the first woman is created. She is taken from man's body; she is clothed by God "in flesh"; she is "bone of my bone"; she and the man are "one body"; they are naked in joy before each other.

Such a description is an extraordinary account of the closeness of God to our bodies and to our sexual nature. It is unfortunate that so much of this is lost in subsequent history and in those spiritual theologies which make the non-physical and the non-sexual the preferred norm.

It is true that the body and the pleasure it gives us can become an object of inordinate and obsessive attention. But it is also true that this disorder is equally present in our "spiritual" faculties of reason and freedom. Indeed more harm may come to the human family from the misuse of intelligence and choice than from the misuse of the body. The body will not allow itself to be abused in an unholy fashion for long without protesting and punishing the violation. The body resists being desecrated. Reason and will, however, are less easily limited in the evil they generate.

I am not suggesting that it is better to be "physical" than "spiritual." Balance is the essence of human development. The body needs special emphasis not only because we have neglected and minimized its importance but also because marriage makes more of the body than any other sacrament.

The sexual aberration and selfish preoccupation, the materialism and narcissism people rightly fear do not come about because the body is declared holy.

16

They occur because people believe they are worthless and their bodies are unworthy.

People accept these notions because of the way their bodies are touched and referred to from the beginning of life. We shall, of course, never get the physical and sexual side of ourselves right so that there are no mistakes in the course of a lifetime. Nor shall we ever get the rational and volitional side of ourselves correct so that all thinking and choosing will be faultless. If, however, the human body is handled as a sacred experience, there is a good likelihood that we shall believe we are worthwhile, that we are sacraments of God and that religion and worship, devotion and awe are rooted in our bodies.

Liturgy and Marriage

All of these points are at issue in marriage. It is noteworthy that the marriage ceremony is the only one of the seven sacraments which gives gender a prominent place. We take "this man," "this woman" to be "husband" and "wife."

Marriage is a sacrament of the human body. The wedding ceremony presents the themes of Genesis and confronts us, as no other sacrament does, with the fact that we are persons because of our bodies.

All the sacraments are physical. One of the great glories of the Catholic tradition is this emphasis on the physical dimension of life. Each of the sacraments takes our body in hand, so to speak, and touches it.

We are washed in Baptism, anointed in Confirmation, nourished in Eucharist; hands are laid on us

17

when we are ill and imposed in the conferral of Orders; Reconciliation requires that we be physically present for the sacrament to be validly celebrated; we cannot be forgiven in writing or by telephone; we must bring our bodies to be absolved.

Indeed, there is more. In the best Catholic tradition, the sacraments are not only celebrated but incorporated in us. "Incorporate" means to embody. The sacraments become ourselves. They are "incarnationalized" in us. "Incarnation" means to embody.

And so we are not meant only to be washed but to wash one another's feet, not only to be purified but to become innocent for others, not only to be baptized but to become Baptism. Christianity is not something one does or receives but something one is.

We are not meant only to be confirmed but to affirm and strengthen others, to be a confirmative presence in the world. We are to call down the Holy Spirit on people and to recognize the Holy Spirit in them. We are to become Confirmation so that people encounter in us the gift or charism of God.

We are not meant only to receive the Eucharist but to enter into communion with God and community with others. We do not celebrate bread and wine but become bread and wine for one another. We are to become one body with Christ, bone of his bone, flesh of his flesh, leaving, if need be, father and mother for his sake. We are meant to be the celebration and the life, the wheat and the grapes, the staff and the chalice of salvation for one another. In marriage, it is a Eucharistic body we bring to our spouse and our children, a body consecrated in Baptism and

Confirmation. Our body was holy from the beginning because God's own hands made us. It will be holy until the end because Christ's love has sanctified and sacramentalized us.

And so it is with the other sacraments. We are not meant only to be forgiven but to become forgiveness for one another, not destined to be reconciled only but to be a reconciling presence in the world. We are anointed not only to be healed but to become healers of others, ordained to lead a community so that we might be led by it.

All the sacraments touch base with our bodies for their validity. Life begins in water and endures only because there is bread; life originates in marriage and continues only because there is healing and forgiveness.

It is all clear and hidden, revealed and reserved. The incarnation shows us God and conceals God. The sacraments declare Christ but do not exhaust him.

In marriage, we give ourselves to each other and never reveal all there is. In the act of love, the bodies of the lovers are hidden from each other at the very point at which they are most naked to each other and most thoroughly joined with each other. The child is hidden in the womb and revealed at birth and then hidden again in the very body that reveals the child to us.

Human life has always been the preeminent sacrament of God's Presence. The body of every human being is the sacramental sign that God is with us. The human body is the only sacrament God celebrated. The celebration has gone on from the dawn of human history.

All history has been a liturgy in which we were the sacraments and God was the priest, in which we were the spouse to whom God made irrevocable commitments. We were the ones with whom God has been most intimate, those to whom God has been faithful since the day we were fashioned. The human body reveals all of this to those who learn how to touch it in reverence.

Chapter Three

Children and Hope
for the World

Children come on the scene in a marriage with personalities and genders we do not foresee, in numbers and at times which elude our planning. It is, perhaps, for this reason that they bring so much hope with them. It is as though they come from another world with a message of hope for this one. They remind even the insensitive among us about the importance of love and tenderness. They bring us bread in the wilderness of despair and lovelessness which may surround us, wine from the grapes of wrath and bitterness.

On this we all agree, that if the world does not care for its children, the world is not worth preserving. Children are the lyric and the music of the world's best song. They justify human existence if any one thing does. They convince each person that there is a fundamental goodness somewhere or else there would be no children.

This is not to say that each and every marriage requires children. Nor is it to affirm that there are a certain number of children each family ought to have. Nor is it to suggest that there might not be good reasons for choosing to have no children.

Nonetheless, the very notion of marriage sets up a special relationship between the couple and children. The etymology of the word "marriage" is rooted in the word for "mother." In the course of a marriage, a couple will be asked frequently about whether they have children and how many, about their ages, names and genders. If the couple has no children, they will often make some comment about this, a comment, of course, that no single or celibate person or even an unmarried couple considers making.

Marriage and Hope

Marriage is founded on hope. To give one's life to someone we know less well than members of our original family, to entrust that person with aspects of our life we withhold from our parents, to identify fully with someone we may never have known through the years of growing and defining ourselves, to do all this with such a person is to risk one's entire future. Lovers hope, sometimes against desperate odds, that their relationship will succeed. And when it does, the reasons for this are unknown to onlookers and even to the couple itself.

It is fitting, therefore, that marriage should have such a special relationship with children. If we are asked which are the best experiences of life, most of us would answer that the presence of love and the gift of children are primary.

People who love so deeply that they give their lives and bodies to each other sustain and inspire us. Children who come into the world with trust and joy, who bring us fantasy and innocence, who make us laugh and care for them are the greatest of all human creations.

Marriage is an institutional form hope assumes; children are the way hope looks when it takes on flesh. When committed love no longer moves us, when children are neither desired nor celebrated, the world will have become a valley of darkness and despair.

We celebrate children but we need not sentimentalize them. Children can be demanding and unruly; they march to different drummers and follow other stars; they arrive unexpectedly and depart unceremoniously; they often compel us to live in their world.

The decision to have children and the number we choose to accept depends upon energy, resources and patience. Children repay us in love and joy that no other human experience approximates. But there is a price demanded for such a gift.

Children, money and sexual experience are three of the most volatile issues in marriage. Children directly affect all three issues. Children do not solve marital problems. They enhance stable marriages and accelerate the decline of faltering ones.

The key to good parenting is the same as the key to friendship and marriage, namely, participation. The more we participate in the life of another, short of forsaking our own autonomy, the more we are bonded to that person.

Children are no different. They compel us to live in their world because they need us there. They require our fidelity to them. They want our bodies and our hearts near them. These needs remain whether the child is five or fifteen or fifty.

Children need us to be parents but they also want us as friends. They came into the world because we were once friend and lover to someone. They require for their future life the same elements of friendship and love which initiated their life in the first place.

Raising children is more demanding than other friendships but not different. The same elements apply. Children are more difficult because they are with us for so long a period of time and through so many stages before adulthood is achieved. But as with other relationships, if we share in the lives of others, they give us their lives in return.

Jesus told us that a seed cannot develop until it loses itself in the earth. When it is buried, it surrenders its former existence and flourishes into a new life. The loss is gain. We do not prefer the seed to the flower or the wheat or the grapes.

The sexual experience in which seed is sown in the body of a woman is a symbol of the death that gives life to the couple and the marriage. Later, children become the fertile field in which the seed of a couple's former life is cast so that a new life of parenting may emerge.

Children change the identity of the couple forever and forge bonds that are never broken. There may be former husbands and wives but there are no former fathers and mothers. The bond is so permanent that parents who lose a child grieve for a lifetime even if it be a child they never brought to birth or a child they knew but a few days before its death. There is no relationship in life except that between parent and child in which grief lasts so long for someone we hardly knew. A parent may never have seen a child or spoken with a child yet the loss may cause pain for a lifetime. There is majesty and mystery in the life a child embodies.

The bond is a reciprocal one. A child who does not know its parents may search for them for years. I have known men and women in advanced age who still wept because they never saw the face of their mother or father. Some people, especially in old age, long for death in the hope that they might see their parents again.

The first home we know is the home our parents make for us. The powerful emotions associated with mother and sister, with father and brother, with love and trust are developed from our home life. Religious experiences are also nurtured there. We call heaven home and give God parental names; we consider members of our faith community siblings; we build our liturgical rituals around our memories of birth and death, family meals and festive celebrations.

Marriage is for Children

The world of marriage and children is a world of so much depth and meaning that many lifetimes cannot exhaust the potential of even one family. Perhaps this is why notions of "forever" and "eternity," "infinite" and "everlasting" are so easily associated with marital love and family life. Who would want a life that would never end if there were no people to love, no family to join?

No one takes a marital partner for a day or a child for a week. The words we use as we forge these relationships are words that tell the other:

"I shall be here until death parts us."

"I shall never leave you."

"I do not care to live unless you are with me."

These are words that seem out of place or at least unusual for any other relationship except that of marriage and parenting.

And so we might suggest that every married couple is obliged to make a home for children in the world. We do not mean that children are essential to their relationship but that children would be safe with them and sheltered in their home. When a couple has developed a value system that celebrates children, when they have made a home in which new life is welcome, they have become a couple open to children even if they do not have them. Marriage ought to be child oriented even if there are no children in it. Even heaven, we are told, is filled with those who have become like little children.

The world is a lonely place when people become too old for children. If one of the greatest joys of young life is children, grandchildren are the crowning glory of later life. I do not mean by this that people ought to be primary caretakers of children when their

26

physical, emotional, financial or mental resources no longer permit this. I do mean, however, that a significant dimension of our life is the care of new life.

When we cease to become the shepherds of new life, we lose our own future and begin to live in the past. If the bond between parent and child is powerful, the bond between the elderly and the young is tender and touching. The elderly do for the young things that parents cannot accomplish. Just as we are parents in some way even without children as long as we have made a place for them in our heart, so we are grandparents of the young even if we have no grandchildren of our own.

This brings us to the last and most crucial point in this discussion. The reason why children are so important is because they help us to be children. Children make the child in us return or preserve the child who is already there.

Friends are friends because they become like each other in significant ways. A person's friends enable us to know what that person is like.

Children make us like them. They remind us of our vulnerabilities and dreams. They show us how easily we can be hurt and how instinctively we run for someone to heal us. They reveal to us how much we want life to be joyful, how playful the human spirit is, how hard it is to destroy trust in us, how ardently we long for love.

A battered child returns again and again to its parent in the hope that this time, perhaps, love will happen. The child refuses to believe a parent is loveless. Every child who finally accepts the evil of a parent hides its face, its shame, its anger. It has been dealt a savage psychic wound. It is as though the child feels that if love is not given by a parent, then all life is a humiliating experience in a hostile environment.

Children make us children. They coax us to talk a language of playful nonsense, to rattle toys that make it difficult for us to remain solemn, to sing songs when we have no tunes, to meditate when we see them sleep at night.

Children are love on the run as they greet us at airports and train stations. They lead us to drop our packages and our burdens, our schedules and our self-importance as they leap into our arms.

As children make us children again, they render the world safe for the very people who brought them into it. The protected protect the protectors. If there were no more children, the world would become an orphan, lose its heart and die of old age and despair.

And so when God came to us, he came as a child and the world was enchanted with the Christmas story. When God was a child, there were stars and angels, mangers and magi, gifts and shepherds, sheep and song, a young man and a young woman very much in love. It was a splendid night. A night to be remembered for as long as time and memory last. God became a child to make the child in us permanent.

When the child became a young preacher, he called God "Abba," a tender word used by children to address their father in Hebrew families. Jesus was child enough to call God by an intimate name.

The young preacher became the greatest story-teller the world ever knew. The world has been changed more profoundly by his stories than by any others.

One has to be a child to tell a story well. The young preacher never grew out of childhood. One day Jesus was asked what heaven was like and who was there. Is it any wonder that he reached for a child, put his arms around him and told us that heaven was open for everyone who becomes a child?

Chapter Four

The God of Leisure, The Christ of Laughter

We never take anything seriously unless we have a sense of humor about it. When we are at home with something, we find it easy to be humorous. To be at home with something, however, means that we have absorbed its meaning and become identified with it so that we are able to be playful.

We are not very relaxed with people we do not know well. And so we pretend to take them seriously. The effort exhausts us. Conversation is artificial and contrived, arbitrary and tedious. Attempts at humor are forced.

There is no state of life in which people take each other more seriously than in marriage. It is, therefore, ideally suited for humor. Indeed, no marriage grows unless each partner finds the other humorous.

Humor derives from respect for the other, from love, from the conviction the relationship is secure. Humor is totally different from ridicule. Ridicule is a sign that one has contempt and that no relationship is desired. Since humor is relational, it is something we share in the presence of the other. Sometimes we delay recounting a humorous incident until people we care for are present. Ridicule, however, happens just as well, often better, in the absence of the other. Humor is grace; ridicule is a weapon.

Humor is a reciprocal experience. If both partners do not enjoy it, it is not humor. Ridicule is a solitary experience. If the other shares in it, it loses its force.

Humor is a great mystery. Only human beings have a sense of humor. Humor has something to do with our essential humanity. When our humanity is under intense pressure, humor becomes difficult or impossible:

Our humanity is under siege when our rational and emotional control is lost. One of the surest signs of mental health is a sense of humor. The insane and the hysterical may laugh but it is laughter with no humor. Such laughter chills the bone rather than warming the heart. It is a hollow, empty, threatening laughter because we cannot hear humanity in it.

Our humanity is under siege when our physical resources are depleted and when we are near death. If humor occurs at such moments, onlookers immediately begin to hope that the person may survive. It may, however, be the last human touch, the last link, the last shared experience with the dying friend.

Our humanity is under siege when we are so locked in sin and darkness, so obsessed with our own selves, so intent on exploiting others that humor is impossible. The laughter of an evil person has no mercy in it. It is laughter with no compassion, the laughter of the heartless and the hopeless. There is no humor in Dante's hell, in Homer's world of the dead, in Virgil's realm of deceased spirits.

Humor, however, enlightens hope and is illumined by it. It derives from the fact that we are not defined by anything limited. We transcend all our limitations and look back on them in amusement. It is easy for us to see the incongruity between things as they are and the other forms they might take or ought to take.

A sense of humor actually has something to do with our religious nature. If we believe in God and in the meaning of existence, if we believe that life never ends and that love has a purpose, then there is no ultimate tragedy. Life becomes a divine comedy.

We can be humorous with our own ineptness because God expects no one to be perfect. Perfection is for the faithless. Perfection is an achievement; it is the result of controlled behavior; it is a solitary accomplishment; it is not the way of the heart or the life of the spirit. We do not expect perfection from people we love and trust. Perfection is an obstacle to relationships since relationships are not built on strengths alone but on vulnerabilities.

Humor is an insight into our transcendence. We are made for another world as well as this one, for further life beyond the one we have begun here. Humor means that we are aware of this in some way, that we can rise above all shortcomings and reversals, that we are free of all constraint.

Humor and Marriage

One of the gifts each spouse can give the other is the gift of humor. Such a couple has no fear for their marriage or each other. They rise above grief and agony and contact the joy in their relationship, the tranquillity in their being together.

There are many reasons why humor goes out of a marriage.

In some instances, the couple trusts their resources rather than their relationship. They begin to believe that money and prestige, housing and comfort, youth and beauty, intelligence and success are essential. They believe in these resources in direct proportion to their inability to believe in each other.

It would be utopian and naive of us to suggest that a marriage without work and income, shelter and opportunities, medical and educational advantages is not under intense pressure. Nonetheless, many of these benefits are missing because the couple stops believing in themselves and becomes locked into insecurity and despair.

One can make too much of resources in a marriage, whether one is referring to a superabundance or a deficiency. In both cases, the humor goes out of a marriage because people become conscious of all that surrounds them but not of each other.

It is prudent to delay marriage until a couple has access to the basic necessities their culture requires for citizenship in it. We must realize, however, that trust in each other is not enhanced by accumulating resources. There is something grim and humorless about abject poverty; this poverty is frequently beyond the capacity of the poor to avert. There is, however, something grave and ponderous about great wealth or the ardent desire to accumulate it. This wealth is frequently chosen over the relationship and creates distance and suspicion. Such a couple is frequently conscious of money inordinately and chooses to be preoccupied with it.

Leisure and Marriage

There is another reason why humor goes out of a marriage. The couple trusts work rather than each other. Leisure with another person is a celebration of that person's value.

We work easily with a great variety of people. Even though we have little choice about those with whom we work, we manage. Leisure, however, does not go well unless trust governs the relationship. Work can be effective even if we have only a superficial tie with other people; leisure presupposes a more substantial compatibility.

It is often said that marriage is work, hard work. There is truth in this observation. Marriage, however, at its best, is leisure. It is sheer joy in the other's presence, whether that joy be exuberant or quiet, sexual or intellectual, cultural or practical.

Marriage is a leisure experience and, in this, it is like contemplation. Contemplation is joy in the presence of life, awe in the presence of the universe, wonder in the presence of God. Contemplation is not really hard work. It is cultivated leisure.

Marriage is a contemplative experience. It is meant for joy and leisure, for awe and wonder.

The finest moments in a marriage are the leisure moments. Honeymoons and anniversary dinners, silver and golden celebrations, talks by the fireplace and evenings under the stars, listening to each other and making love, reading together and praying side by side.

Work is important in a marriage. It too is a bonding element. Caring for a house or a career, for a child or the future is hard work and contributes to the relationship. But it is leisure which celebrates the relationship and rescues it from agendas and schedules. Leisure lets each person know how worthwhile each is even when not productive. No amount of order in a house or income in a family convinces people of their worth as fully and unforgettably as the leisure moments they spend together.

Leisure is an act of faith in each other. Work is something we all must do in a marriage. There is social and legal pressure to force it upon us if we are negligent. Leisure, however, is intimate and cannot be compelled. It is a gift well given, the substance of memories, the basis of hope, the guarantee of love.

Work is oriented to a task even though we do this task in a personal way with another. Leisure, however, is for the person. There is no task. There is only time to be given and presence to be shared. There is no greater gift to offer since time and presence are our richest and scarcest resource.

As people trust each other, they find significant leisure time. Leisure, like life, is created by love.

The couple now begins to laugh together as leisure and humor nourish each other. It is the laughter of people who know that they count, the humor of warmth and conviction, the joy of intimacy and fidelity.

Faith overcomes solemnity. Humor convinces us that life is not an obligatory experience but an optional gift. Life's prime obligation is that we enjoy the humanity we have been given and the people with whom we share it.

Beyond the Couple

Another reason why humor goes out of a marriage is the confinement of trust to the couple itself. Trust is a value that is intended to be shared with everyone who does not make trust foolhardy.

The couple grows when it trusts a future not of its own making and the whole human enterprise, when it believes the world is a good place to be and the present century a wonderful time to be alive. The farther out the couple's trust goes with others, the more enriched their trust becomes in each other.

Religious faith, at its core, is an affirmation of trust in the whole process. It declares that we do not despair in our sins or lose hope in the face of death.

Religious faith trusts God to care for the marriage and for the couple in a way the couple cannot care for each other.

Religious faith is not the same as church attendance, nor is it identical with moral behavior. These are values but they are not faith. Faith is a commitment of the human heart to God who guarantees its safety. Faith is a relationship, not an obligation. It is a surrender to life, a conviction that life is never destroyed and that it, therefore, eventually prevails.

Faith frees us for humor. It assures us that all does not depend upon us and it allows us leisure in the world.

Jesus must have had a wonderful sense of humor. No one that free could be humorless. No one could win the affection of so many people unless that person had a sense of humor.

Christianity enriches marriage by encouraging the couple to receive the Gospel and trust life. The Gospel begins with Christmas music and ends with Easter melodies. It does not evade the hard work or the awful tragedy of life. But it tells us that life begins in joy and ends in meaning. A couple who grasp this vision become tranquil in the deepest recesses of their hearts and souls.

The least pragmatic things we do are often the most practical. A marriage is not made meaningful by resources and work, by planning and techniques, by shelter and security, by income and prestige, by possessions and career. A marriage is made wonderful by the visions the couple engender in each other's heart.

A life-giving marriage is surrounded by humor and leisure, by faith and trust. As the years go by, the couple learns to count not their possessions and promotions, their savings and success. They count instead the good times spent laughing, the good times when they were alone, the good times which seemed to have neither beginning nor end because they were always at the heart of marriage. The good times outlast and outnumber the losses and the anguish in a successful marriage.

At some point in every marriage, one spouse must let go of the hand of the other for the last time. Other partings may have been painful but this is the worst. The memories of all the times those parted hands were joined again are not enough to lessen the devastating loss which now engulfs the surviving spouse.

It is faith and trust that now sustain us. If there was a time when the one we loved never existed and yet found us and held our hand, is it foolish to go on believing that the pattern will repeat itself? We shall find our lost love and join hands once more. Our deceased spouse took the leisure and the laughter we shared into another world. Since that was the best of us, we know that, while we await our reunion, our life companion will not be left alone.

Chapter Five

Rituals and Memories

Life is linked together by the simple rituals of everyday living. As we surround ourselves with rituals, life is humanized, enriched, and made memorable. A marriage is filled with ritual from the wedding day forward; the cycle of a marriage is a liturgy of love.

A ritual is a set of symbols which enable us to deal with life and celebrate it. Rituals are not necessary, in the strict sense, but they create an environment in which life is honored and developed.

A few examples may help this to become less abstract.

There is a simple ritual for dressing and starting the day. The selection of clothes and the order in which we put them on, the combination of colors, letting in or keeping out the morning light, the choice of breakfast and where we eat it, the use of silverware, the arrangement of plates and glasses, the departing of the house, the farewells and final reminders, all these and more form a ritual.

If we consider this list of rituals, we notice that each action is not necessary and somewhat arbitrary. It could all be done another way but we choose to do it in this manner. The choice makes life easier and it helps to define us.

The rituals we follow also make a statement about how we regard the people with whom we live.

Ritual and Healing

When human life is depleted, rituals have the power to restore us. One of the things I suggest to people when they are severely depressed or shattered with grief is to go on with the simple rituals of life. It is important that they do these themselves even though others may offer to do them.

The way we wash a cup or arrange a flower, the rituals of shopping and setting a table, the decoration of a cake and the lighting of candles in a house, the more elaborate ceremonies of Christmas trees and Easter eggs, of Thanksgiving dinner and July fireworks a remarkable capacity to heal us, to pull us back into life. The life force in the ritual revives us; the fact that we do things not only for ourselves but for others enables them to become part of our life once more.

Even when we are not wounded, ritual pours life into us. The great events in our life story would be diminished if they were not ritualized. We lose something irreplaceable if we make a wedding day a day like any other.

Conversely, we can be burdened rather than liberated by ritual. If we make the ritual of a wedding too elaborate and theatrical, too commercial and expensive, the ritual engulfs rather than supports the event. Too much ritual is depressing and tiresome. It takes the human warmth out of the ceremony.

The love of the couple and the life commitment they make is the essence of the wedding. The more this is lost sight of, the less meaningful the ceremony becomes.

The anniversary of that wedding ought to be ritualized. When cards and gifts, notes and dinners, candles and kisses, flowers and leisure, gratitude for the past and promises for the future, lovemaking and music are considered unnecessary and intrusive, the marriage suffers a loss. An anniversary is not like any other day.

The list of these events can be extended. Birthdays and holidays, seasonal changes and project completions, baptisms and house warmings are enriched and made unforgettable by ritual. Many years later, we can still hear the songs and see the faces, remember the words and recall the gifts, relive the joy and rekindle the love these rituals expressed.

Home as Sanctuary

Home is like a church or a theatre. Although it is primarily a private place, it is also a sanctuary for the most crucial ceremonies of life.

More meaningful ritual occurs in a home than in any other place in the world.

The rituals of each day's beginning and of each

day's ending are ritualized. The way children are read to and tucked in, kissed and blessed, touched and assured that the night will not harm them, that daylight will return, that the aloneness of sleep will be accompanied by the presence of the mother and the father in the house, all this and more form the everyday rituals of family life.

We cling to these rituals as children and remember them all the days of our lives. I have read to and tucked in dying adults, kissed and blessed them, touched and assured them that death will not harm them beyond repair, that daylight will return, that the loneliness of their journey will be healed by a God who awaits them as a parent, by family members who precede them and, soon, by those of us who remain a short while longer.

In the course of a year, it is remarkable how many rituals are performed in a home. All the greetings and farewells, all the meals and festive days, all the colors and ribbons and lights, all the singing and the sorrow, all the parties and the prayers make the home a sacred place. All the lovemaking and the life, the promises and forgiveness, the arrival of new-born children and the final departure of those we did all the rituals with, these make the home holy ground.

Moses took off his shoes in the presence of God. Every one of us might remove our shoes as we enter a home because we have been invited to a holy place. God is in every room, present to the life that goes on there, filling the home with the peace created when friends and lovers dwell together in harmony. There is no other place we are more human than at home, no place where we turn to more readily when holidays are to be celebrated or when life has injured us and we need healing.

There are, of course, other things which go on in the home. There are hostilities and sometimes physical abuse. There are angry words and broken promises. There are shattered dreams and loveless hearts.

We are especially saddened when we hear of these because the home is the last place they ought to happen. When these sorrows afflict a family, rituals of forgiveness offer hope. No family flourishes unless its members frequently request and receive forgiveness. It is only when forgiveness is denied that the marriage is dead.

Forgiveness may even be postponed and the marriage lives. Sometimes we must respect the emotions and the timing, the ritual and words someone requires before forgiveness can happen with a free and a full heart. There are times when we must wait and not rush the moment when someone who was injured is willing to forgive.

There are more religious experiences, more spiritual victories, more sacramental encounters in a home than occur in a church. Home is a temple and cathedral, a church, where the rituals of love and the liturgy of life are endlessly reenacted.

Home as Theatre

There has always been a close connection between theatre and liturgy. Both use symbols and words, sight and sound to help us participate in a life which is not our own. The home which, as we have said, is a church is also a theatre. Life is staged in a home, not in the sense that it is fantasy and artificial but in the sense that it is dramatized and invites participation in it.

Even from the earliest times, when human beings lived in caves, they decorated their homes with paintings and pebbles, with beads and bones, with furs and flowers. A home that is bare of decoration is depressing. It is a wonderful and necessary work to make a home a place where the dream and the liturgy of life can be lived. The fact that men as well as women now share in this liturgical action of ritual and drama is one of the most creative developments of our time.

Ritual and Repetition

Ritual, by its nature, does not tire us in its repetition. When ritual becomes obsessive and impersonal, it wears us out and robs us of life. This is not ritual, properly speaking, of course. When ritual is done only because it is obligatory, it becomes rubrics and imprisons the human spirit.

Few things are more suffocating than religious ceremonies one attends only out of obligation. They are as oppressive as birthdays or anniversaries, civic events or holidays which are endured because one is socially obliged. We speak of going through the motions. It is a mechanical and dreadful experience.

Ritual, however, does not tire us or trap us. Kisses and gifts, Christmas and Easter, weddings and baptisms follow patterns or scripts. There is something expected as well as surprising in them. And yet they are never so familiar that one gains no further life from their repetition. Indeed, we become concerned if we sense no joy in their presence.

Christmas carols and Easter music, birthday songs and anniversary celebrations are predictable and enchanting at one and the same time. No matter how familiar something is we never exhaust its mystery if it has meaning for us.

A home is a place where people decide that Christmas and birthdays, anniversaries and Easter, holidays and holy days will never go uncelebrated. For when the music stops and the candles are extinguished, when the flowers wither and the lights go out, when there are no more parties and festivities, the home becomes a tomb rather than a sanctuary, a house of darkness rather than a theatre of light.

When the ritual stops, the life of the family ends. Even in the concentration camps and the prisons, people broke bread and sang songs; they went to their death with prayers and melodies they learned at home as children; they called out the names of loved ones as they died and reached for them. In the ritual and the memory, life went on and prevailed even as it was taken away. Only when there seemed to be no point to the ritual did hope itself perish.

Ritual as Etiquette

There is a particular kind of ritual we call etiquette. These are gestures of courtesy and convention which are frequently undervalued in what they contribute to a marriage.

The etiquette of meals and how we dress for them, the condition in which we leave rooms, the names we use for each other, the holding of a door, the refusal to take telephone calls when at table, letting others know when dinner will be delayed and why, whether others will come to dinner and why one may not be home on time, these courtesies are not profound rituals. They seem almost inconsequential in their significance. And yet the absence of these in the life of a family diminishes our capacity to care for one another. Over the years, it has a withering effect on relationships.

We are, of course, conscious of people who are so polite that they are formal, so attentive to etiquette that they become controlled and impersonal. Politeness can be used as a weapon to keep others at a distance or to make them feel uncouth. This is not the etiquette of which we are speaking. Etiquette, properly utilized, helps other persons know we care and are respectful of them. It creates an environment in which people feel worthy and valued.

Memories and Hopes

The rituals we perform in the days and years we live with those we love make the marriage a source of memories and hopes. Everything seems possible with a man or woman who celebrates us and our relationship.

Indeed, even Christmas and Easter, Passover and New Year become associated in our memories not only with God but with the people with whom we celebrated them. We ourselves become part of the Christmas story and of Easter glory. We find that the rituals are not only the celebration of a distant God or an ancient time but a celebration of the present and of the people who surround us.

God takes on the faces of those we love and yesterday becomes this moment. The past gives the present a future. God finds a place in the midst of this great mystery we call our family. God attends the liturgy in our domestic church and invites us into the dance of life. God becomes brother and sister, mother and father, friend and child.

God breaks bread at our side and takes new wine, holds our hands and makes love to us, colors the flowers, calls us by name, lights the candles. Indeed, we are on holy ground when we enter a home. It is a privileged place, a sacrament, a temple and a cathedral, a sanctuary for life, a shelter for love.

As years go on, the memories become so rich and so many, the stories become so numerous, the traditions so plentiful that the marriage and the home can hardly contain them. And so we pour them out to those who will one day take our place. The children ask us why this night is different from all others or when we were married or how we fell in love or when they were born or what it was like when someone we loved died in our arms.

We find life again as we remember and they find

hope in the enchantment that surrounds their listening. The rituals and the memories will one day be enshrined in other homes when ours is vacant.

One day we shall go on to another home, one Jesus assured us he had gone ahead to prepare for us. We shall remain here, however, even after death, every time Christmas is celebrated and wedding rings are exchanged, every time candles are lighted and names are remembered.

The generations and the centuries go on but they enrich the ritual and make it more venerable. Each of us is part of this circle of love. One day someone held our hand and told us we were loved and began a circle which was never broken. The simple gesture was a ritual but the memory of it and the life in it lasts forever.

Chapter Six

Careers and Money, Commitments and Frugality

Marriage is a surprising combination of romance and practicality.

Love is not an efficient experience. And yet, paradoxically, families are the most efficient units in society. When other agencies attempt to duplicate what families do in the normal course of things, the cost and complication are crushing.

Preparation of meals and housecleaning, birth and dying, child care and nursing for the elderly, sleeping and leisure activities become enormously expensive, impersonal and sometimes depressing when bureaucracies manage them. Love is often lacking and always less personal as a public service.

We are not suggesting that many of these institutions do not do their best or that dedicated people do not work in them or that they do not bring benefits they alone provide. There are times when families simply cannot cope. We are saying, however, that the family is the model and the norm, the preferred place for all of us, the most humane institution human history knows.

It is ironic that public services are developed for efficiency and yet involve a great deal of waste. Families are not formed with efficiency in mind and yet conserve energy and resources.

Love and Structure

Love happens in a structure even though it eludes all structures. There are rules to play by, assigned by gender or inclination, by choice or convention. There is a specific place one lives, routines of work, rituals of understanding, decisions about children, provisions for eating and sleeping.

Love does not develop in a wilderness but in a cultivated environment. Love is an intimate rather than an outdoor experience, most often a private rather than a public event. Love needs to be housed and restricted; it requires boundaries and parameters; its mathematics, in the beginning, is limited to two people, and later to a few family members. In the context of this circumscription, love becomes universal and reaches out for the whole world.

Even though love is efficient, it becomes nonetheless expensive. Careers and money may not be the sum and substance of love but they are not incidental to the process.

If homemaking is sacred and central to marriage, work outside the home and careers also play their part. The point of work is more profound than the making of money. Although this income allows a couple to function, there are prior values in work and careers which need to be addressed.

Careers are usually a means by which a family joins the larger community. No family is, in its own right, an autonomous culture. It needs the completion which comes from involvement in the social task.

Work, furthermore, is important because it is more than something we do. Work is an expression of ourselves. We are realized in the projects we undertake for the welfare of others.

Work is not a punishment or a discipline, a burden or a curse. It becomes this when people are used for profit, when human beings become merchandise for others, when men and women are made to labor in environments which assault their essential humanity.

In its nature, however, work is a mystical experience, setting up a relationship between the work we do and the product we produce, between ourselves and the others who work with us. We identify ourselves not only by name but also by occupation. We frequently feel an immediate connection with strangers who do the same kind of work we do.

Careers become problematic when the marriage becomes incidental to the demands and dynamics of the workplace. In most marriages, even with the shortened hours and work week of the modern age, more time is expended traveling to and from the workplace, working away from home and in work brought home than is spent on the marriage itself.

Careers may become so absorbing that the marriage is deemed a liability. We can take each other so much for granted that we think everything else is more important. It is a pattern repeated with depressing frequency. There is even social and cultural support for this distortion. Families are often honored for their affluence and occupations rather than for the character of their relationships and the quality of their love.

This absorption with work rather than people is a form of idolatry. We worship the task rather than respect the person. God made human life a unique image and likeness of the divine. Idolatry in the modern age is not so much a formal neglect of God but an indifference to persons.

Careers and money can become addictive. They may lead people to frenzy and neurosis. The mystical experience of work creates madness in those who do not strike a balance between the need for money and the necessity of relationships, between the demands of their careers and the desire for love. No one dies wishing he or she made more money or spent more time at the office. People, at the end, look at the faces and hold the hands of those they are about to leave and wish they had more time with them.

Marriage and Tranquillity

Marriages can profit from contemplation and reflection, from meditation and value clarification, from journal keeping and personal prayer. There are times in the early morning or late at night, alone in a car or traveling in a public vehicle, while dressing or bathing when people ought to take stock of their lives.

Contemplation rescues us from frenzy and madness. It makes us know that careers are valuable and that marriages depend upon them for development. But this is true only if community and relationship, marriage and love, spouses and children are given the time and attention they deserve.

Money may be an asset or a demon. It is an asset when it liberates life from unnecessary burdens, when it allows creative leisure and fosters opportunities for human relationships. It is a demon when it possesses our souls and makes insatiable demands. People seldom believe they have enough money, no matter what the amount. There is always someone richer, someone with more so that we are able to be exceedingly affluent and feel perpetually deprived.

Money becomes addictive as we require greater and greater amounts to satisfy an ever diminishing sensitivity to its pleasure. As with any other addiction, we come to sacrifice everything for money and do things for money we once thought we would never countenance.

As money accumulates, we begin to suffer insecurity. Money was supposed to make us secure and now we find ourselves suspicious of others and threatened by the loss of wealth. Life becomes so unthinkable without vast resources that we contemplate crimes or even suicide if our assets dwindle substantially. Enormous reserves of time and energy, emotion and life investment are devoted to money management. We surround ourselves with security systems and move into neighborhoods where wealth is so conspicuous that they are likely to be burglarized.

We are not suggesting that money is evil or that poverty is not terrifying. We are noting that money demands a price from us in human terms and that it seldom brings the benefits we anticipate. It is most useful when it is kept in perspective. Money easily homogenizes reality, assigning everything a market value, drying up the sources of creativity and diversity which liberate the human spirit.

Money and Human Resources

The more we are invested in people the less money we need. It sounds banal to comment that the best things in life are free. The banality, however, is based on an important truth. The possessions we purchase are valuable and useful only if they are prized less than those gifts which have been freely given. The presence of another person and the love of a child, the grace of God and the sacraments of Christ, the seasons of the year and the stars in the heavens, faith and friendship, music and poetry give life human shape and substance.

Commitment to people leads to creative frugality. By frugality, we do not mean impoverishment but personal enrichment. A certain distance from possessions enhances our humanity and enables us to appreciate the worth of others.

Frugality means that we use what we need but that we do not accumulate those things which blind

us to people and suffocate values. In a consumer society, the assumption is that more material goods create more meaning. The good life is defined in terms of
possessions, many of which we do not need and all of
which require time, attention and care. We sometimes
purchase things to prove to others that we are worth
noticing and that they are not.

As we become committed to people, we need less
of the things money buys. Love rescues us from idolatry. Love's contemplative dimensions create frugality and peace.

If a couple becomes a consuming couple, the marriage itself is eventually consumed, reduced to merchandise and bartered for goods and services that are
not worthy of it. The entire theory of consumerism
rests on the notions that life is surrounded by scarcity
and that commitments limit life. We might discuss
each of these ideas in turn.

The assumption that life is a scarce commodity
prompts people to accumulate enormous resources.
We become identified with what we own, defined by
it, so that we are eventually possessed by our possessions.

There is fear that unless we have it all, we have
little. We assume that our life is diminished if we have
less than we might.

Life, however, is an inexhaustible experience.
There is abundance everywhere. Scarcity occurs, for
the most part, in those exotic and artificial items which
are not necessary. Indeed, scarcity in these areas is fos-
tered so that frenzy increases and market values climb.

Love, however, cannot be depleted and life itself

is superabundant. The universe is vast and the mystery of our own planet is more than we can fathom. If some of our brothers and sisters do not have enough to eat or a place to live, if they are without clothing, medical care and education, it is not because there is not sufficient for everyone but because a few refuse to share from the very abundance which has become humanly useless to them.

Some, however, choose to live simply so that others may simply live. This frugality, however, is not even done for this reason alone. Frugality does not mean only that we restrict our ownership and consumption so that there will be more for others. It means, more profoundly, that we neither want nor desire artifacts which assault human life and oppress its spirit.

Commitment, furthermore, is seen by some as a road to impoverishment and deprivation. The assumption is that if we remain committed to a few values and a few people, if our options are limited, we wind up with less.

The truth of the matter is different. A life with no commitments does not open the world to us but closes it. We rush from experience to experience in the desperate hope that we might find peace.

Many of these experiences might bring us peace but fail to do so because we seize them rather than letting them unfold. When we approach reality acquisitively, it loses its capacity to settle us. We plunder life rather than live it. We do not remain long enough to know the meaning of that which we rush by and even destroy in our haste.

Devotion and Mystery

A human person is deeply mysterious. We must be patient a long time before many of the melodies of a human life are played. We must be composed as the other composes the music and harmony of our relationship. We must be attentive with the attention only the contemplative, the frugal and the committed possess.

Jesus once told us that when we find a pearl of great price we devote ourselves to it. Marriage is a pearl of such transcendent and inexhaustible worth that it is fitting to devote a lifetime to its keeping.

There is hardly a man or woman alive who is not moved by the devotion one human being may have for him or her. This devotion, however, must not be taken for granted or received as our due. It must not be a pearl, in another image Jesus gave us, that we cast before swine. It ought not be, in another Gospel reference, the seed we scatter in the brambles and thorns of the careless life we live. It must be cultivated in the good soil of our love. When devotion has been squandered and a marriage is lost, a great pearl is forfeited and we lose the light that might have been reflected on us from it. When devotion is cast away, weeds rather than wheat come from the earth. In the betrayal of every human relationship, an act of treason is directed at the whole human family.

In still another biblical instance, Jesus told us that possession of the entire world is not worth the loss of the human spirit. If we had abundance beyond calculation, all the prestige and affluence one life could hold, all the kingdoms of the earth at our disposal, this would matter little if we squandered along the way the devotion of a loving man or woman or of a needful and happy child.

The leaving of a great fortune to a family seldom does them much good. Bitterness is often intense in the settlement of a large estate.

The great gift to leave behind if we wish our children to flourish and our spouses to have life again is the gift of devotion and commitment. If they remember us as those who thought their life worth our life, then they will know they were pearls of great price. If we leave, not a large fortune, but the memory of our devotion, they will never exhaust it. It will yield a hundredfold in the soil of their hearts.

There is no one who cannot die devoted. Such a person immediately lives again in the life and memories of those to whom he or she gave everything. The first lesson of life is learning how to give the last measure of devotion.

Chapter Seven

Failure and Forgiveness

No matter how well we plan, something goes wrong. There is simply no way for us to sustain perfection, to express love with no flaws, to give without sometimes becoming selfish.

Every marriage has built into its texture the threads of integrity and the tears of infidelity. We are not as faithful as we wanted to be. And so the music of marriage is sometimes muted and melancholy. Love has sad songs to sing.

One of our responses as we reflect on our relationships is to wish they were different in many ways. And yet, if they were, one wonders whether they would be better.

Love is seldom more extraordinary than it is after forgiveness. St. Paul once commented that God has so ordered human history that when something goes wrong even greater good comes from it. St. Paul did not mean that we ought to do evil or become complacent about it but that God creates goodness even out of our misdeeds. It is a consoling thought.

We are able to hurt most deeply those we love most profoundly. Sometimes we inflict pain without having been aware of it, even while intending good, in circumstances that turned out differently from what we had expected.

The invitation we offer another to enter our life, the willingness to receive someone else's life in return is an invitation to become happy together. It brings with it the inevitability, however unintentional, of suffering at our hands. We are destined to be healers of one another from the very injuries we ourselves caused. Each of us is a wounded healer who brings to the other our brokenness and our wholeness.

Sometimes the pain inflicted is so deep and so frequent that it is not only one or the other who is harmed beyond repair but the marriage itself which is dealt a lethal wound. We shall discuss this later in this chapter. For the moment, let us focus on wounds that heal and on our desire and capacity to heal them.

The fact that we disappoint each other rescues our marriage from becoming a closed system. If we could be everything for someone, we would need no one else. We might not want to have children; there would be little room for friends and no reference to God. The creative resources of marriage, however, are renewed and multiplied by children, by friends and by God.

There is sterility in human self-sufficiency, and unexpected impotence in human omnipotence, a loss of transcendence in attempting to be divine ourselves. The disappointments bring our marriage into the public forum as we search for others to fulfill us; the inadequacies draw us out of self-containment into self-donation. The fact that others can do for our spouse things we cannot accomplish brings the rest of the world, so to speak, into our marriage. Self-donation is not only a way of surrendering ourselves to our spouse but a way of releasing our spouse to others for help they alone can bring.

We may ask the mother or father of our partner to give his or her son or daughter life again when we cannot; we may need a brother or sister, a friend or professional to heal with sibling affection, companionship or therapy the person we entrust to his or her keeping. At other moments, we call upon God, formally and forcefully, to come to our assistance, to make haste to help us, to be the parent of this marriage and nurture it back to life.

We stand in poverty before those we love. We have at times only a widow's mite to add to the treasury of love. On one occasion, Jesus multiplied bread in the desert because there were so few loaves and so much need. On another occasion, he provided wine at a wedding because the resources of the couple were depleted.

Sometimes our spouse requires from us the bread of life, the wheat of love, and we have not enough loaves to nourish the need. It is then that God multiplies for us the very poverty we bring so that there is an abundance not of our own making. Those who rely on God and turn to faith for strength attest to the miracle of life's capacity to renew itself and to flourish a hundredfold from the seeds of insignificance.

Sometimes our spouse seeks from us the wine of

a sufficiency we do not have. In our inadequacy, God gives the increase and replenishes us with cups of gladness and vessels of joy. Those who turn to God when they are depleted attest to the fulfillment God gives, to the emptiness God restores.

The multiplication of bread in the desert is described as a party; the provision of wine at the wedding is a festive occasion. There would be no parties or festivities if we were self-sufficient. In receiving we celebrate not because we receive our due but because we have been gifted with more than we deserve.

We celebrate Christmas and Easter not because we earned them but precisely because we did not. We celebrate birthdays and anniversaries because people entered our lives with the miracle of their presence from worlds beyond our control. Love does not claim it has a right to what it receives.

The poor, for the most part, celebrate more exuberantly than the rich. This is also true of those who know they are spiritually poor. The awareness of deficiency intensifies festivity. We rejoice that our emptiness has been discounted by grace.

Sources of Festivity

In a marriage, we find two powerful sources for festivity. Both of these derive from our inadequacy.

In the first place, we are conscious of how little we have to give. The joy comes from the fact that this is frequently enough.

It surprises us that our arrival home is enough to

cause happiness in our family. Marriage seems to expect everything and to be satisfied with much less.

It humbles us that our poor words are transformed into poetry in the hearts of those who receive them. It startles us that the slightest things we do generate gratitude and that the least efforts at love are abundantly rewarded.

Marriage offers endless reasons for festivity for those who sense their poverty. The truth of the matter is that we may be more adequate for each other than we realize. Each time we become aware of this, we rejoice. We do not even know why it is that we prove adequate. It seems to have little to do with us. Even when it does, we seem to do less than the response we receive justifies. In time we come to know that it is the other who makes us sufficient.

And so we rejoice, not for ourself alone but because together, as a couple, we have made significance out of our mutual poverty.

What do we do to deserve the life of another? We know how grateful people are when we save their lives. Physicians and firefighters, police officers and ministers attest to this. People who rescue others from drowning or who pull friends from burning buildings, people who give shelter in hurricanes or earthquakes witness to this. The saving of another life is a transcendent experience because each life is valuable and mysterious, inexhaustible in its capacity for good and in its future potential.

And yet, in marriage, someone offers us a life, a life not in danger of dying so that we rescue it but a life freely given and given not for a day but for as long as one lives. Who is worthy of this? Who dares to declare that such a gift can be earned? In marriage, we are grateful because another saved and preserved our life. When they make us aware of this, we sense the transcendence and joy of having rescued someone we love.

In the desert, we are given bread. In the wilderness, there is wine. On the road of life, we find a Good Samaritan. When we perish from lovelessness, a father restores with his loving embrace all we had lost in our prodigal waste. Just as we carried to the grave our only son, a young Rabbi, a storyteller from Galilee, touches him, gives him life and places him in our arms. When we wept for the death of our only daughter, Jesus calls her by name and gives her back to us.

We deserve nothing and we seem to receive everything. And so marriage is a celebration of our poverty and of life's abundance, of our mortality and of God's might, of our sin and of divine salvation, of our hunger and of infinite compassion, of missed chances and miraculous cures. Out of our failure to be more, fidelity is born. Fidelity is impressive because faithlessness was possible. In the forgiveness we are given, a future is fashioned for us when we thought there was none.

There is another powerful reason for festivity in marriage. It derives from the fact that strangers, so to speak, arrive to help when we are unable to provide. By strangers, I do not mean those we do not know at all but those we did not know could help as much as they do.

Our failure to become all we would like leads us to celebrate others who come on the scene. They arrive like magi from some unknown land, willing to follow the star of our marriage. And they come with gifts we could not afford, gifts which celebrate the marriage and bring life.

They arrive like shepherds who leave their sheep and their own concerns to attend to us, shepherds who give us their time and their presence so that we might not think no one cares. They arrive like Easter angels who tell us the marriage will live again or like women who come to the tomb with healing oils and abundant perfumes.

Jesus once described heaven as made up of strangers who gave others clothing and shelter, comfort and nourishment as though they were members of our families. Jesus tells us they were our unknown brothers and sisters. Indeed, he reveals that he himself had joined our family circle as a brother even though we did not at first recognize him.

If Jesus had been self-sufficient, the magi and the shepherds, the angels and the women, the strangers and the Samaritans would have added nothing. If our marriages are self-contained, all these are neither wanted nor welcome. And we lose not only the healing and the gifts but the life and the festivity. Imagine the joy which would never have been realized if the magi were turned away and the shepherds kept out, if the angels were not heard and the women were not needed, if we preferred to do without all the strangers brought us.

Marriage and Divorce

We ought not conclude this chapter without making some reference to divorce.

There are some unforgivable sins in a marriage. I do not mean by unforgivable that either spouse has the right to withhold pardon or that anger and vengeance are endlessly justified. I do mean that the marriage itself may not be able to forgive the sins committed against it. Just as the human body can withstand assaults against it as long as these assaults are not in any one instance lethal and as long as these assaults do not cumulatively collapse the immune system, so a marriage endures until a fatal wound or a series of offenses makes further life impossible.

The end of a marriage in divorce may be the saddest song the world knows. It is worse than death in many ways because death is not a rejection but an inevitability. It is foreseen on the first day of the marriage and referred to in the wedding vows. Divorce, however, is not expected. It batters the human heart and inflicts a trauma from which we never fully recover. It seems unnecessary and appears as something which might have been avoided. It is pain, we assume, which need not have happened. Death comes to all marriages but divorce seems cruelly to have capriciously selected our marriage for destruction.

Sometimes divorce is fully justified. This justification is realized only if we are willing to forgive our former spouse and also ourselves for something neither really wanted. At an earlier time in the relationship, it seemed impossible. And now, no other alternative is available.

At such a time, it is important to believe that God does not withhold forgiveness. It is crucial to understand that all marriages fail to some extent in terms of what they might have been.

The divorced must know that strangers and friends will heal them. The world is filled with magi and shepherds; the angels and the women have not gone away. Festivity will not be denied us. God will not take bread from our mouths, wine from our hands. We shall be fed again by love although it seems at times we shall starve to death.

The final act of forgiveness in many marriages occurs when we ask for pardon on our deathbed. We ask the other to forgive us for leaving, to absolve us for dying, even though the parting is not of our choosing. Marriages seem to have been made for arrivals, not departures and here we are in a final farewell.

In this last goodbye, we need to be forgiven by our faithful lover for not having made more of ourselves, for having been bold enough to receive another life into our keeping in marriage when we could hardly manage our own.

At such a moment, forgiveness passes into gratitude. And we find that in our dying breath our faithful lover has given us another reason for festivity.

Chapter Eight

All That Is Freely Given Is Never Lost

Happiness is built into the structure of marriage. Sharing life with someone we love is the highest priority in the life agenda of many people. Giving life to another human being is perhaps the most noble thing we do. Sexual love is one of the most joyful of human experiences. The list could be extended but already we can see how marriage is meant to bring happiness. These three values of sharing life, giving life and sexual love are cited in Genesis as made by God for marriage.

Even when marriage is distorted and becomes little more than obligation and propagation, happiness frequently occurs. Marriage is so embedded with a personal character that it brings joy and meaning to people even in those centuries and cultures where role models are rigid and pressure to marry derives from considerations other than the welfare of the couple.

The untold stories of heroism and love between married people are one of the great glories of human history. Even today when we are tempted to become cynical about life and pessimistic about its future, we can become hopeful by reflecting on the impressive devotion and sacrifice operative in most families of the world. In counseling, one often meets people whose self-forgetfulness and commitment are inspiring even though they themselves take little note of it.

It is unworthy of us to focus only on the problems of marriage. It is easy to sensationalize the physical, sexual and substance abuse in marriages and families, to concentrate on selfishness and hostility, to emphasize consumerism and neglect, infidelity and divorce.

These problems are clearly present and in numbers that do not allow complacency. The agony in this breaks the hearts of children and victimized spouses and even of counselors and friends who feel the anguish and are often unable to stop it. We would be superficial and insensitive if we discounted the pain and the desperation, the desertion and the devastation of lives some marriages leave in their wake.

There is, however, little likelihood these problems will not receive sufficient attention in our day. The opposite may be true. We may concentrate on them so endlessly that we begin to assume they are the norm. There are even those who gain satisfaction by dwelling on the misery of marriage.

Nonetheless, most marriages work out well. They are sources of joy not only for the couple but also for the children and the families joined in law or united as grandparents.

Marriage has the most impressive implications for human growth and spiritual enrichment human history has discovered. We are honored as a race by the fact that we made marriage a goal of human life and that we supported marriage with religious, cultural, social and legal resources.

Some of the disillusionment which accompanies a discussion of marriage occurs because we overlook what a massive undertaking it is. To commit oneself to live fifty or sixty years with another human being, to share the satisfactions and sorrows of another life as well as one's own, to raise children with their different personalities and varied demands, to earn the income for shelter, nourishment, clothing, medical and educational needs, to watch those we love suffer and even die, to feel uncomfortable about one's own illness because it creates burdens for others, to do all this is to accept in life almost more than people ought to be expected to manage.

And yet, these experiences are part of most marriages at some point or other. People handle these challenges with bravery and even lightheartedness. They find energy to contribute freely to volunteer work, to assist needy neighbors and family, to care for disabled parents and siblings, and to celebrate the rituals of social and religious life.

People tend to discount the sacrifice entailed in all of this, to confess guilt for not having done enough, to hide their burdens and to assume a carefree manner before their acquaintances.

In all of this, we have the ingredients of nobility and beauty. Only God knows all the details of these magnificent and hidden stories, all the notes of these impressive and private melodies. One day, when human history is over, we shall hear the epic of human goodness. And we shall weep in astonishment at the magnitude of it all, at the sheer and unalloyed goodness of billions of people who toiled and celebrated through the centuries and who wished they could have done more.

When we marry, we enter this great company, this congregation, this global family of married couples who brought more grace and dignity to human history than it could hold. We are honored because so many good people have been here with their love before us and because so many good people surround us now with their devotion. We dishonor them if we forget this, if we trivialize it, if we demean what has been accomplished by concentrating only on the problems and the failures, the heartache and the grief.

Genesis tells us that God saw us after we were made and thought of marriage first as the grace we would be given before all others. God structures marriage in a relational manner. The first man is lonely and God creates a companion for him. The first couple is made inseparable, bone of bone, flesh of flesh, and yet they are different as man and woman. The bonding is not only physical but psychological as they cling together and forsake all other relationships to foster this one. Sexually and spiritually, they become one body and one life.

The grandeur of the description of the first marriage is breathtaking in its scope and beauty. The people who wrote these brief passages were aware of the problems of marriage. Immediately after this description, those very problems are cited, problems of pregnancy and tyranny of one spouse over the other, problems of hard work and death itself, problems of shame and guilt, of betrayal and the fall.

And yet the opening chapters of Genesis are a lyric, rejoicing in the goodness of marriage. God gives marriage to us before religious institutions and ritual. This may be due to the fact that marriage so easily makes us religious and that God is clearly present in a relationship so filled with life and love.

Marriage is a different relationship from all the others we form. There are four elements which encompass this uniqueness. A word about them might be useful.

Sexual Love

The element of sexual love distinguishes marriage. We are, of course, not naive. A good deal of sexual expression occurs before marriage and outside marriage. Yet there is a consensus in the human family that sexual expression has a privileged place in marriage, that it is more physically and humanly satisfying there, that it requires a lifetime for its development and that marriage assures this.

Even in our permissive and candid society, the notion of sex outside marriage is regarded as startling. One does not gossip about a married couple having a sexual relationship. Indeed, the opposite is true. If a married couple does not have a sexual relationship, the couple hides this and it becomes an object of concern. People are ennobled when someone chooses them as a lifetime sexual partner and easily exploited when someone asks them for a short-time sexual affair. Marriage and sexual love, therefore, have a compatibility that no other relationship or arrangement approximates.

Children

Another element distinctive to marriage is children. We are aware that some marriages exist without children. We know also that children are sometimes born to people who are not married. Marriage, however, is the privileged environment for children. Although marriages exist without children, this is not the general norm and expectation. Such marriages are frequently without children not by choice but because of some necessity. In any case, if someone had to place children, that person would look instinctively for a married couple. Marriage and children go naturally together.

When there is a sexual relationship between an unmarried couple, children are seldom wanted. Even though this relationship approximates marriage in many ways so that it almost duplicates it, even though the couple consider themselves married and judge their sexual relationship responsible and ethical, even though this relationship lasts longer than some marriages and is known to all, the couple rarely desires children. Children complicate rather than enrich the relationship in most cases.

The opposite is true in marriage. Not only are

children expected, they are the object of longing. A married couple often regrets that there are no children. This is sometimes a source of disappointment for others.

Children place burdens on a marriage but most would agree they enrich it. Children flourish best in marriage even when the relationship is far from ideal. They seldom do better in public institutions even when these institutions provide more benefits than children receive in a troubled marriage. Even these institutions see their work as temporary and secondary. They consider the placing of children in stable homes the best advantage they can give children.

Not only do married people want children for the most part but children want their parents to be married. Marriage is the best environment for children, who are among the best experiences life provides.

Comprehensiveness

A further element defining marriage is comprehensiveness. There is no relationship in life that touches so many different aspects of our existence as marriage. In marriage, almost everything about us undergoes change. The law and society define us differently. We are expected to be, not alone, but with our spouse on important occasions and in day-to-day living. People do not look for our close friends or parents or children to be with us as much as they look for our spouse when we are on the scene.

In marriage, our bodies and our time, our homes

and our finances, our names and our roles are mutually shared.

The comprehensiveness reaches into other areas of life. We generally tell our spouse everything about ourselves or approximate that totality. We confide in marriage truths we keep from others. Not only is this generally done; it is even presupposed. A spouse who learns of significant information which a partner revealed to a friend or even to a parent but not to the spouse is usually offended. The withholding of such confidence is often a sign the marital relationship is troubled.

I do not intend to say that one ought to reveal so readily that nothing may ever be kept to oneself. There are times, furthermore, when problems are confided more effectively in religious, therapeutic or medical settings. Some information might offend one's spouse or damage the relationship needlessly and permanently.

The point of the withholding in these instances is not so much that the spouse has no right to know but that the timing may be wrong or the maturity of the relationship not yet sufficiently developed or the amount of harm or worry caused would not be justified.

Marriage is the most comprehensive of all relationships.

Permanency

The final element in defining marriage is permanency. We know that many marriages do not last and that some of them should not. But all marriages begin with the hope of permanency. Legal systems do not envision time limits when marriage is contracted; social custom and religion reinforce the ideal of permanency.

We move away from parents and friends, from family and even children. We leave neighborhoods and church communities we have lived in since birth. We change careers and nationality. All of this is taken in stride or not unexpected. It causes sadness but no one sees it as a tragedy or an aberration.

When one moves away from one's spouse, however, we immediately conclude that something has gone wrong. There is shock and grief. As mobile as our society is, it does not envision the moving away of one spouse from the other.

The wish of those who care for us is that our marriages flourish and that, even if all else changes, we shall remain together as a couple until death parts us.

These elements of sexual friendship and children, of comprehensiveness and permanency define marriage as a unique relationship. Every one of these elements involves sacrifice.

There is probably no life experience where sacrifice is so meaningful. There is a proportion in marriage between sacrifice and life, between selflessness and love. To this extent, marriage is a Christic and a Eucharistic event.

No one in history has brought more life and love into the world through sacrifice than Christ. The Eucharist is the central Christian ritual for recalling this sacrifice and for entering into communion with the life and love which flow from it.

In marriage, the couple is the bread broken, their life together is the wine poured. Each is communion for the other; each can say to the other, "This is my body, this is my blood, for you."

Marriage is a vocation. It is an invitation from God to fulfill whatever destiny is ours.

It is not as fundamental a vocation as that most basic and essential of all vocations, to become the person we are summoned to be, with the unique gifts and individuality that involves. It is not a vocation that is so specified in its expression that one has the right to claim that the spouse one marries is the spouse God intended.

Yet if God has called human beings to anything, it is to marriage. It is sacred and religious in its core not only because God was so immediately involved in its fashioning but also because the future of everything human depends upon it. Indeed, God may be revealed more clearly in marriage than in any other setting.

Marriage is consecration. All that is freely given to it is never lost but transubstantiated into life and love. The sacrifice in marriage is part of the liturgy of love, a liturgy which renews memories of Christmas in the birth of children and of Easter in the belief that love is stronger than death. Marriage is the wheat and wine of life's liturgy, a religious calling in which we pass over from self-centeredness into a community of affection, a passage which brings us out of ourselves through our families to the heart of God.

Chapter Nine

We Shall Meet Again

In Scripture, there is probably no more tender and beautiful statement of marital and erotic love than that found in the Song of Songs. The book is, in reality, a collection of five love poems about the personal and sexual longing of a young married couple. It is, at times, so graphic in its description that some timid spirits have been offended by it; it is so unashamed in its equation of physical love and spiritual meaning that some have reduced it to symbol and analogy as a way of neutralizing it.

The achievement of this particular book is its ability to fuse the mystical and the sexual. It makes sense on the sexual level but it also works if one interprets the bride's longing for her husband as the soul's longing for God. It is a book which helps complete Genesis.

Genesis describes sexual life in mystical terms: bone of bone, flesh of flesh, leaving father and mother, one body, one life. Indeed, these themes are transferred into Christological references in the New

Testament where Jesus gives us his flesh in the Eucharist, where discipleship is described as leaving father and mother, where we are invited to become one body and one life with Christ.

It may well be that sexual experience is most meaningful in a mystical atmosphere. There is a significant difference between genital lust and sexual love. Lust is promiscuous and satisfied by anyone; love is personal and fulfilled by fidelity.

Conversely, the sexual metaphor has been used often by mystics to describe their experience of God. Mystics employ marital terms for God. They write about ecstasy and surrender, union and rapture.

The journey together of a couple in love through the years is a mystic journey.

Biblical Mysticism and Sexual Symbols

The Song of Songs is erotic without ever becoming obscene. It affirms the body without neglecting the spirit. It is thoroughly sexual and completely relational. It reflects in this the qualities of a good marriage.

The author of the New Testament Letter to the Ephesians finds Christ and the Church in the bodily experience of marriage. Sexual submission is presented in ecclesial and Christological terms. As husband and wife give themselves to each other and become one body, so Christ and the Christian community give themselves to each other in the body of the Church. It is all very sexual and very mystical, very physical and very spiritual, very graphic and very sacramental.

Marriage may be the primary sacrament in the Catholic liturgical system. Marriage is a sacramental celebration of intense friendship and comprehensive love. It generates everything that has final significance for us: human life and faithful love, the world as we know it and the Church as a community.

A marital couple once brought the Son of God made flesh into history. The bond between Mary and Joseph must have been passionate as well as pure or else it would not have been much of a marriage.

The Hebrew Bible begins, in Genesis, with God's creation of marriage. The Christian Bible begins, in Matthew, with a marriage and the birth of the Christ child from it. The holiness of the first couple begins the human race; the sanctity of Mary and Joseph brings the human family its ultimate meaning.

It is difficult to imagine what greater value revelation could declare for marriage. Scripture repeatedly cites marriage as central to God's love for the world. It is the keystone of the bridge bringing divine and human life together in harmony.

Although the Catholic sacramental system is an impressive one, it has not been available to people through most of human history and, even today, reaches only a percentage of the human race. The central sacramental symbol which has been with the human family from the dawn of its origins and which has immediate reference to virtually everyone today is marriage and sexual love.

Of the seven sacramental signs, marriage is the

only one found clearly in all cultures. The shape of marriage, its essential symbolic value, is appreciated and celebrated around the world. It is difficult to be in any culture and not feel the joy and participate in the happiness weddings bring. Marriage is the pivotal holy event in the lives of most people; children become the mysterious and overwhelming sacraments of God's presence in families throughout the world.

The central sacrament of God's grandeur is marriage. It brings the world reverence and devotion, awe and wonder, grace and love in categories all can understand. A man and a woman, hand in hand, arm in arm; a couple expressing affection and embracing; a mother feeding a child at her breast; a father cradling his son or daughter—all are universal symbols of humanity.

We may see other signs and rituals and feel estranged from the people and culture which enact them. We are not, however, distant from the signs we have just enumerated. They are rooted in our bodies and hearts. We feel part of the intimacy and fidelity of such love; we ardently wish it to succeed. For we know that when such love flourishes, all the world lives. We find ourselves in every couple and see in their countenances the face of humanity itself.

Nourishment and Eucharist

There are three natural experiences in which the human body is penetrated in the normal course of events. Each of these occurrences leads to miraculous transformations. Life is transubstantiated through

81

them into new forms of human presence and communion.

The first of these is eating and drinking. We take bread and wine into our bodies and these become our flesh and blood. The body must be open or vulnerable, if you will, to take in nourishment. There must be, furthermore, joy or hope in us. People stop taking sustenance when they are grievously ill or severely depressed.

The most elaborate and meaningful rituals of life tend to be organized around festive or religious meals. Bread and wine become hope in our hands as we choose to go on with life by our willingness to receive them. The miracle occurs as we become the very bread and wine we take into our bodies. The hope symbolized by all this takes on flesh in us.

Words and Transformation

Another penetration of the human body occurs in listening. In order for us to hear the word of the other we must allow its sound to enter our body physically. As our ear receives the word, it resonates inside us. We make it ours by our reception of it and by entering into communion with it. The word of another person must become incarnationalized in us for us to hear it. It enters us and we give it flesh.

Language may be the most distinctive thing we do as humans on the physical level. Each of the human senses is surpassed by some form of animal life. There are animals who see or hear more effectively than we do; they exceed us in detecting scents and touch. We are, however, the only ones who develop words and language. We try to put the best of us into words.

Words convey the mystery of human presence in an utterly unique and intense manner. An example may help. If we discovered a letter from a deceased friend, the reading would move us and put us in contact with the departed person. If, however, we were given an audio tape recorded by that person, the sound of the words would impress us even more profoundly with presence and nearness.

When we speak to others, we become vulnerable. This is why the inattention of others disturbs us even when the level on which we are communicating is relatively superficial.

Conversation, like nourishment, occurs in an atmosphere of festivity and joy. As we become ill or depressed, we restrict our words or cease speaking altogether. The sign that a relationship is no longer desired is the refusal to share words. Even if the words are angry, there is more hope in them than in the stony, dead silence of absolute rejection. When those we love die, it is the ability to speak to them that we lose first of all.

When we allow the word of another to enter our body through hearing, we receive that person's presence. As that word becomes enclosed in our body, we become united with that person. Relationships are nourished by the bread we break with a friend and by the words we share.

We are changed intellectually and spiritually by the words we take in just as we are transformed physically by the nourishment we receive.

When Jesus is portrayed in the New Testament, it is in terms of bread and words. We are consecrated as we enter into communion on these levels.

Jesus is bread for the world. More intimately, he calls the bread he offers the disciples his very body.

Jesus is the word of life, the Word of God made flesh. He invites us to receive his word and keep it, to be changed by it and to offer it to others.

There is mystery and miracle at every turn in the process of ordinary living.

As people fall in love with each other, they organize their special friendship around the rituals of shared meals and protracted conversations. The intimacy of these two experiences is profound. The meals are arrayed with flowers and candles, with bread and wine, with color and music. The same elements are utilized in Passover celebrations and Eucharistic liturgies.

The couple speaks to each other in secluded places, hand in hand, on long walks and in scenic settings. They offer each other their presence and their life through sacramental signs of devotion, with bread and words. They consecrate each other with their love and create communion between them with their life.

Sexual Symbols and Life

Bread and words, consecration and communion lead to sexual love. The body is again penetrated for life and transformed on powerful physical and spiritual levels. Sexual bonding requires vulnerability just as nourishment and words did. We eat and speak in joy and we are meant to make love in festivity. When people are ill or depressed, the lovemaking ceases just as the meals and the conversations do.

In sexual love, the most miraculous transformation occurs. Conception is a transubstantiation from elements of relative insignificance into a human person. In this penetration, it is not only the couple which is renewed and the marriage that develops but a new human being who comes into the world. The sexual communion of lovers opens them to the transcendent dimensions of love, reveals them as life-givers and makes them sacramental signs. Their bonded bodies are sealed with a spiritual force which fuses them into a creative experience they initiate and God brings to fruition.

Just as it appears impossible that bread will become our body, just as it seems unlikely that the words of another will bring their presence into our flesh, so it is an unfathomable mystery that a human person will be born from sexual passion and physical union.

The new person emerges from our bodies with life it seems we never had. The new person is at once from us and beyond us. The child takes nourishment and shares words, just as we once did. But there is also laughter and dancing we never taught and poetry and music we never learned ourselves.

In these three penetrations, our vulnerability and our significance are revealed. We become Eucharistic sacraments as bread and wine are transformed into life, as words are transformed into presence and relationship, as sexual love is transformed into community, the future and new human beings.

Intimacy and Immortality

When one partner dies, that person takes into another world a personality shaped by the bread we broke together and the words we shared, a personality shaped by sexual love and the children born from this. Nourishment, conversation and passion are sacraments of intimacy and signs of immortality. When communion between the couple is so complete, the absence is only an interlude. The couple is not so much separated but made expectant for reunion. The absent partner is not gone but awaited in a new way. It is Advent season in their relationship.

Jesus shared bread and wine during the Passover meal he celebrated before his death. He then went away into the land of death. The disciples who received him as bread and kept his words saw him again on Easter morning. At moments, they were uncertain if it was truly he until he broke bread and called them by name. They encountered the memory and the presence of him in those intimate actions of communion he did so well.

Jesus was born from a marriage in the Christmas birth which ended the Advent vigil. He comes to life in the body of Mary in a marriage filled by the love of Joseph. The Son of God is born not in a temple or in a priestly aristocracy. He is born not in an atmosphere of liturgy or law, institution or religious structures. He is born where marriage happens and love is generated between a young man and a young woman. The Creator God of Genesis made marriage in the beginning; the Son of God came to birth in a marriage when the world needed a second start and an ultimate meaning. Jesus becomes the Christmas child who will later become the Passover Messiah and the Easter Christ.

Marriage reenacts the creation of the world when marriage was God's first thought. It renews the liturgy of grace and salvation which gives us Christ. Married couples enter into the Christmas mystery by the children they bring into the world or by their special relationship to children.

Married couples share the Passover experience of bread and words by creating homes which serve as a sanctuary for these. They pass over by these symbols into the life of each other and into the grace of God.

And so it is fitting that the lovers, who kept Christmas and Passover alive in their homes, will one day share an eternal Easter together. We believe as Christians that the absent lovers will be united again and that death will be taken away. For death is a lesser bond than the bond of love.

Nothing shapes our life more tellingly than love. As the years of marriage accumulate, each spouse shapes the other by love and becomes inseparable from the other who becomes precisely who he or she is because of the marriage. We are what love makes us.

When death severs a marriage bond, one spouse goes into eternity with the other's love intact. The first spouse to die takes the remaining spouse to God because the two of them remain inseparable at a profound level of their life. The spouse who remains keeps forever the shape and character of love left by a lifetime of devotion.

Death is no real parting. The resurrection of the body begins not on the last day but on the day of death. Once hands are joined, the circle remains unbroken if love is not withdrawn. God once allowed the first man and woman to take nothing out of Eden except each other. It is the ultimate grace God gives us. God never takes away from us those we have loved.

In another land, in an everlasting home, the lovers will break bread and share words. They will touch each other's bodies and see, as the disciples did, that the wounds of death have been healed. And they will know each other in an even more marvelous way. Even lovers are unaware of how much goodness is in themselves and in the other. They will call each other by name again and they will finally become all they wanted to be to the other. There is no better way to say this than to declare that the marriage will make them happy forever.

ALSO BY ANTHONY T. PADOVANO
produced by Paulist Press

Christmas to Calvary (book)
Winter Rain: Six Images of Thomas Merton (video)
His Name is John (video)